CW01213189

Original title:
The Secret World of Sleep

Copyright © 2024 Creative Arts Management OÜ
All rights reserved.

Author: Ophelia Ravenscroft
ISBN HARDBACK: 978-9916-90-808-2
ISBN PAPERBACK: 978-9916-90-809-9

Soft Shadows of Night

Whispers weave through the trees,
Moonlight bathes the gentle ground.
Dreams unfurl like soft leaves,
In this tranquil, hallowed sound.

Stars peek through the velvet sky,
Each one a wish waiting to soar.
The night breathes a soothing sigh,
Cradling secrets, asking for more.

Figures dance in the pale light,
Flickers of life, stories untold.
In the embrace of the night,
We find warmth in silence bold.

As shadows blend with the dawn,
A promise lingers from afar.
With every moment, we are drawn,
To the magic of the night star.

Lullabies of the Unconscious

Softly hums the hidden dream,
Where thoughts drift like clouds in the sky.
In the gentle, silent stream,
Restless minds learn to fly.

Cradled deep in twilight's glow,
Each whisper a comforting sigh.
The heart finds peace in the flow,
While the world fades and waves goodbye.

Layers of night softly blend,
Shadows dance with intricate grace.
In this realm, we transcend,
Lingering in a sacred space.

Each lullaby a tender thread,
Weaving memories sweet and bright.
In this place, fears are shed,
As we wander through soft night.

Echoes of Silent Reverie

In the stillness, echoes bloom,
Thoughts float like petals to the air.
Is it night or just a room,
Where dreams linger without a care?

Footsteps trace a path unseen,
A journey beneath the moon's gaze.
Memories drift, soft and serene,
In this world of twilight haze.

Every whisper tells a tale,
Of hearts once lost, now entwined.
In the silence, we unveil,
The treasures that we longed to find.

Lost within this quiet grace,
Time bends like shadows on the ground.
In reverie's warm embrace,
We find the love that knows no bounds.

Starlit Fantasies

Beneath a canopy of stars,
Imagination takes its flight.
Wanderers dream of distant bars,
In the soft embrace of night.

Galaxies spin, tales unfold,
Each twinkle a story to tell.
In the silence, dreams take hold,
Magic breathes a timeless spell.

Visions dance in the moonbeams,
Painting worlds both bright and rare.
In starlit dreams, life redeems,
A tapestry beyond compare.

As dawn whispers its sweet refrain,
Memories linger, soft and light.
In the heart, we hold the gain,
Of starlit fantasies in the night.

Starlight Streams at Dawn's Threshold

In the hush before the light,
Stars flicker in the night's embrace,
Dreams drift softly as they take flight,
With each breath, the shadows race.

Golden hues break through the dark,
Whispers of dawn begin to sing,
A canvas painted with a spark,
Embracing all the hope they bring.

The clouds blush in a tender hue,
As daybreak wraps the world in gold,
A moment fleeting yet so true,
In starlit streams, our dreams unfold.

Dances of Dust and Sleep

Silent rooms in twilight's glow,
Particles dance in gentle flow,
Memories linger, soft and sweet,
In a world where night and dreams meet.

Shadows waltz on creaky floors,
Echoes whisper through the doors,
Each sigh tells a secret fair,
In the silence, dreams repair.

Time drapes softly, a velvet shawl,
Lulling spirits in its thrall,
Dances weaving, close and tight,
In the hush of fading light.

The Lurking Magic of Hypnagogia

Awake yet dreaming, mind adrift,
Veils of slumber gently lift,
Colors clash in shadowed play,
As night's enchantment lingers, sways.

Thoughts meld like stars in twilight skies,
Reality fades, as laughter flies,
Every whisper pulls us near,
In this realm, the strange feels clear.

Fleeting visions dance and glide,
Where dreams and waking worlds collide,
A tapestry both wild and free,
In hypnagogia's mystery.

Chasing Fancies on Silent Wings

With twilight's breath, we start to roam,
Chasing fancies that call us home,
Silent wings brush past our cheeks,
In the stillness, wonder speaks.

Through hidden paths where shadows lay,
Imaginations gently sway,
Each flutter carries dreams anew,
In the scribe of night's soft hue.

The stars bear witness to our flight,
Weaving tales in the cloak of night,
In every heartbeat, magic reigns,
As we soar through the ethereal plains.

Glimmers of Unseen Visions

In the hush of night's embrace,
Soft whispers dance, a fleeting trace.
Dreams awaken with a gentle sigh,
Unseen visions that brush the sky.

Stars are painted on velvet blue,
Each glimmer holds a promise anew.
Fleeting moments, a soft command,
Guiding lost souls, hand in hand.

Sleeping on the Edge of Infinity

Here I lie, on time's soft brink,
Where shadows play, and cosmos wink.
Drifting thoughts in a tranquil sea,
Lost in dreams, just you and me.

Eternal whispers cradle the night,
With every heartbeat, a new delight.
Floating freely, beyond all bounds,
In this space, no end surrounds.

Surreal Sojourns at Dusk

Twilight spills its painted hues,
Crafting worlds with whispered clues.
Each step forward in soft embrace,
A dreamlike journey, a timeless chase.

Clouds weave tales in the fading light,
Stars emerge, ready for flight.
As day retreats into night's arms,
The universe sings of hidden charms.

Threads of Twilight Interwoven

In twilight's glow, the threads entwine,
Weaving stories, yours and mine.
Colors blend in harmony,
A tapestry of destiny.

With every heartbeat, we sew the seam,
Living echoes of a shared dream.
As stars awaken, so do we,
Bound by fate, eternally free.

Secret Paths of the Nocturne

In the whisper of the night,
Footsteps echo soft and light.
Hidden trails beneath the trees,
Secrets carried on the breeze.

Shadows dance with gentle grace,
Every corner hides a place.
Silence speaks in hushed tones here,
Inviting hearts to draw near.

Moonlight glimmers on the ground,
Guiding wanderers unbound.
Each turn leads to a new fate,
In the dark, it's never late.

Lost in dreams where spirits play,
Nocturne sings till break of day.
Paths unknown, yet so familiar,
In this realm, the soul's a chiller.

Reveries in Moonlight

Beneath the glow of silver beams,
The world unfolds in whispered dreams.
Memories linger, soft and bright,
Enfolded in the arms of night.

Glistening dew on blades of grass,
Moments cherished, none should pass.
Time stands still, as hearts take flight,
In this dance of pure delight.

Waves of nostalgia gently flow,
Carrying tales of long ago.
Each sigh breathes an ancient song,
In moonlit reveries, we belong.

Eyes reflect a starry sheen,
Lost in thoughts of what once been.
Underneath this timeless sky,
We weave our dreams and let them fly.

Reality's Fading Fringe

On the edge where shadows blend,
Fingers touch where moments bend.
Reality begins to fray,
As twilight steals the day away.

Softly drifting on the breeze,
Whispers echo through the trees.
Truth and dream begin to fade,
In the dusk, where lines are laid.

Frames of thought, like clouds, disperse,
Traveling where the edges curse.
Fleeting visions start to wane,
As we dance in joy and pain.

In this space, we mold the night,
Chasing sparks of errant light.
Reality a transient thread,
In twilight's weave, we forge ahead.

Shadow Play Beneath the Stars

In the dark, shadows entwine,
Stories lost in night's design.
Echoes pulse through silent air,
A dance of forms beyond compare.

Stars above like watchful eyes,
Keeping guard, they flicker, rise.
Figures moving, cast and drawn,
In the play of dusk till dawn.

Mysteries creep with every sway,
In the theater of the gray.
Curtains rise with every spark,
Illuminating scents of dark.

Reality bends in subtle ways,
As we drift through dreamy maze.
Lost in echoes, shadows play,
Beneath the stars, we find our way.

Whispers of the Midnight Realm

In the stillness of the night,
Soft secrets gently creep,
Moonlight casts a silver glow,
Awakening dreams from sleep.

Through the trees, the shadows sway,
Voices call from far away,
Echoes dance on whispered winds,
As the stars begin to play.

Night unfolds its velvet cloak,
Wonders hidden, tales untold,
Every whisper, every sigh,
Weaves a magic to behold.

Underneath the watchful sky,
Souls entwined with cosmic light,
In the realm where shadows meet,
We embrace the endless night.

Dreams Beneath the Starlit Canopy

Underneath that twinkling dome,
Dreams are born, and spirits roam,
Wishes carried on the breeze,
Floating gently like a poem.

Images swirl in the dark,
Visions sparked by silent larks,
With each blink, a world unfolds,
Crafted by the cosmic arcs.

Candles flicker, shadows play,
In this realm where thoughts can stray,
The universe, a soft embrace,
Guides us through the night's ballet.

Stars are lanterns in the night,
Guiding dreams with subtle light,
In the silence, hopes take flight,
Beneath the starlit canopy bright.

Shadows Dancing in the Dark

Silhouettes that waltz and weave,
In the night, they softly cleave,
Echoes of a hidden dance,
Mysterious, they take their leave.

With a rustle, secrets sway,
In the twilight's gentle play,
Each flicker tells a story old,
In the dark, they find their way.

A tapestry of light and shade,
With every movement, dreams fade,
In the quiet, spirits swirl,
In the shadows, songs are made.

Whispers join the unseen throng,
In the dark, they hum a song,
Bound together, lost, and found,
Shadows dance where we belong.

Lullabies of the Moonlit Hour

Cradled under twilight skies,
Softly hum the night's replies,
Moonbeams weave a gentle trance,
Where the weary heart complies.

Hushed are all the worldly sounds,
In this peace, true solace found,
Each lullaby a whispered prayer,
Resonates through starlit grounds.

Embers glow in silver streams,
Filling hearts with tender dreams,
As the night wraps us in care,
Painting life with gentle themes.

In the moonlit hour we rest,
Finding solace in our quest,
With each note, we drift away,
Held within the night's soft chest.

Hidden Realms of Rest

In quiet corners, shadows play,
Whispers of peace drift softly sway.
Underneath the willow's guard,
Time stands still, the world is marred.

Gentle breezes brush the ground,
In this haven, solace found.
Moments linger, golden light,
Filling hearts with soft delight.

A tapestry of night unfolds,
Wrapped in warmth, each secret holds.
Echoes hush, the stars align,
In hidden realms, the soul will shine.

So close your eyes, let silence bloom,
In whispered dreams, dispel the gloom.
Here in rest, the heart can mend,
In hidden realms, all sorrows end.

Driftwood on the Ocean of Dreams

Lost on tides of glistening blue,
Driftwood dances, sailing through.
Each wave tells of journeys far,
Guiding hope like a distant star.

In the embrace of whispering foam,
The heart finds a place to roam.
Secrets carried from shore to shore,
In every splash, a tale to explore.

Beneath the surface, currents weave,
Ties of wonder we can't conceive.
Floating softly through the night,
Dreams illuminated by lunar light.

From every grain of sand that clings,
In driftwood waltz, the spirit sings.
On the ocean of dreams, we float,
Together in this buoyant boat.

Murmurs of Midnight

Under silken skies, stars confide,
Murmurs of midnight, softly glide.
Secrets nestled in the breeze,
Whispers flow through ancient trees.

Shadows dance on silver streams,
Carrying the weight of dreams.
As time slows, hearts align,
In the hush, our souls entwine.

The moon reveals a tender grace,
Illuminating each hidden place.
In the quiet, moments tease,
Tales of love, carried with ease.

When the world begins to sleep,
In its silence, a promise keeps.
Murmurs of midnight, sweet and low,
Guide us where the wild hearts go.

Surrender to the Night

Embrace the darkness, let it in,
Where shadows breathe and fears grow thin.
In twilight's arms, surrender slow,
Find the peace that night can bestow.

Stars alight like scattered pearls,
Dancing softly, the cosmos whirls.
In stillness, let the chaos cease,
A gentle whisper brings you peace.

Close your eyes, the world retreats,
In quiet corners, solace greets.
Breathe in deep, let worries fade,
In the night, the heart's unmade.

Surrender fully to the night,
Where every shadow holds a light.
In this moment, feel the sway,
As dreams guide you on your way.

Beneath the Surface of the Mind

In depths where silence weaves its thread,
Whispers of thought, softly spread.
Fragments of dreams begin to stir,
Echoes of life, they gently confer.

Hidden currents flow like a stream,
Carrying shadows, a distant gleam.
Every flicker of light from within,
Tales untold, where memories spin.

A labyrinth spun from hopes and fears,
Where laughter mingles with silent tears.
The subconscious sings its haunting tune,
Beneath the veil of the silvered moon.

Exploring realms both rich and vast,
Holding the future, embracing the past.
Through tangled paths, we seek to find,
The secrets dwelling beneath the mind.

Oft-neglected Corners of Night

In darkness drift forgotten dreams,
Where silence reigns, and quiet gleams.
The stars above hold stories tight,
In oft-neglected corners of night.

Lost in shadows, whispers play,
Forgotten wishes fade away.
A flicker here, a shadow there,
Crafting tales that float in air.

Moonlit paths, where doubt has crept,
And secrets lie that time has kept.
Softly calling from the abyss,
In midnight's cradle, we find our bliss.

To wander through each hidden space,
In solitude, we find our grace.
Embracing stillness, we ignite,
The magic of the corners of night.

Ebbing Tides of Hypnosis

Waves of thought crash and retreat,
In a rhythm soft, where dreams entreat.
The ebbing tides caress the shore,
Whispering secrets, forevermore.

Drifting deeper into the flow,
Letting go of what we know.
In gentle pulls, reality bends,
As consciousness weaves and transcends.

A lullaby sung by the sea,
Inviting the mind to roam free.
Awash in calm, the senses blend,
As tethered thoughts begin to mend.

In this trance, where time suspends,
Awakens the soul, a journey that wends.
To explore the depths, to boldly dive,
In ebbing tides, we feel alive.

The Palette of Sleep's Realm

In hues of night, the colors flow,
Crafting dreams in a silent show.
Soft strokes of slumber brush our sight,
A canvas spun from shadows bright.

Tints of blue, and whispers of gold,
Stories in whispers, quietly told.
A masterpiece woven in a sigh,
As the stars paint stories in the sky.

Textures of velvet, deep and rich,
In every corner, a new niche.
The palette blooms, impressions blend,
In sleep's embrace, where visions mend.

Awake or dream, which is real?
In vibrant hues, we softly feel.
Each night a journey, grand and surreal,
In the palette of sleep's wondrous wheel.

Melodies of a Dreamtime Wanderer

In shadows of the evening light,
The wanderer's heart takes flight.
With whispers soft and secrets deep,
He dances where the night winds sweep.

Underneath the silver moon,
He hums an ancient, timeless tune.
Stars twinkle like forgotten dreams,
In the quiet, nothing's as it seems.

Each step falls like a gentle sigh,
Echoes where the lost ones lie.
With every melody that flows,
The heart of night, the wanderer knows.

Embracing shadows, he will roam,
Through twilight realms that call him home.
In the tapestry of dusk and dawn,
A dreamtime dance that lingers on.

Artifacts of the Dreamweaver

In the attic of forgotten dreams,
The weaver gathers light it seems.
Threads of silver, shades of blue,
Whispers of past and futures too.

Each artifact with tales to tell,
Of morning sun and evening bell.
Woven into fabric fine,
The stories blend like aged wine.

With every stitch, a life unfolds,
In tangled knots the dreamer holds.
Fragments of hope, despair, and glee,
Artisan of all that's yet to be.

The dreamweaver with gentle grace,
Takes time's essence to embrace.
Creating worlds both near and far,
In the gallery of who we are.

The Gossamer of Nighttime Prose

Through gossamer threads of night,
Words fall like stars, soft and bright.
Each sentence dances, whispers low,
In twilight's grasp, we ebb and flow.

The prose unfurls in silken hues,
Painting shadows, binding views.
In hidden corners of the mind,
The stories seek, in silence, find.

In the hush where secrets thrive,
Imagination springs to life.
Each page turned, a sigh escapes,
Unraveling dreams in gentle drapes.

Nighttime's muse, with tender care,
Crafts the words that fill the air.
In every line, pure magic flows,
The gossamer of nighttime prose.

Flowing into Endless Dusk

As daylight fades to muted hue,
A stream of twilight dances through.
Time drips slowly from the sky,
In vibrant whispers, days slip by.

Mountains bathed in amber light,
Underneath the blanket of night.
The horizon blends, a gentle kiss,
To cradle dreams in tranquil bliss.

In this space of ebb and flow,
The heart finds solace in the glow.
With every breath, the shadows sway,
As dusk weaves tales for night and day.

Flowing gently, shadows cast,
In the present, future, past.
Embracing all that time bestows,
We find our peace where twilight grows.

Veil of Nighttime Whispers

Stars shimmer soft, like secrets shared,
The moonlight dances where shadows dared.
In the quiet hush, stories unfold,
Tales of the heart, both timid and bold.

Breezes carry murmurs, sweet and low,
Crickets sing softly, in twilight's glow.
Each sigh of the night, a gentle plea,
A tapestry woven, by dreams set free.

Misty thoughts linger, elusive and bright,
Guiding lost souls through the velvet night.
In every corner, the echoes reside,
Whispers of memories that time cannot hide.

Embrace the stillness, let worries take flight,
For in the veil, we find our delight.
The night holds magic, wrapped tight in its arms,
A haven of solace, cradling our charms.

The Other Side of Dawn

Horizon blushes, a promise unfolds,
A new day awakens, as darkness scolds.
Through morning's mist, the world comes alive,
In the warm breath of light, we learn to thrive.

Birds greet the sun with cacophony sweet,
Nature's orchestra playing, a rhythmic beat.
Each ray spills hope, painting skies with grace,
Inviting lost dreams to find their place.

In the stillness before the day breaks,
The heart whispers softly, as courage awakes.
Embrace the unknown, take a step near,
For on the other side, the path becomes clear.

Embellished with colors, the day stretches wide,
Time waits for no one, it urges, it guides.
With every heartbeat, new journeys commence,
Dare to step forward, in the dawn's evidence.

Remnants of a Faded Dream

In twilight's grasp, shadows start to fade,
Whispers of wishes, in silence cascades.
Fragments of laughter, like petals they drift,
Carried by time, as memories shift.

A tapestry woven with threads of the past,
Moments we cherished, too fragile to last.
In the echo of night, a sigh finds its place,
Remnants of dreams linger, a soft embrace.

Each glimmer of hope, a flicker, a spark,
Chasing the darkness, igniting the dark.
Though visions may wane, their essence remains,
A haunting reminder of joy mingled with pain.

In the garden of thought, where dreams intertwine,
We gather the pieces, as stars brightly shine.
Though faded and worn, they whisper our name,
A treasure remembered, in life's gentle game.

Elysium Beyond the Eyes

Beyond the horizon, where colors converge,
A land of enchantment, where dreams emerge.
With every heartbeat, we venture so near,
In the realm of the soul, where visions are clear.

Mountains stand tall, like guardians wise,
Whispers of wisdom float under vast skies.
Rivers of joy weave through valleys of green,
In Elysium's heart, our spirits convene.

Each moment is gold, wrapped in timeless light,
A sanctuary found, through day and through night.
Through laughter and tears, love's tapestry spins,
In the depths of our hearts, the journey begins.

As stars fade away, and dawn starts to rise,
We find our true selves, in the vast, open skies.
Elysium beckons, a promise so bright,
In the tapestry of life, we find our true light.

Clocks that Forget to Tick

In a room where silence reigns,
Time hangs heavy like a shroud.
Dust dances in the golden beams,
Moments lost in a fading crowd.

Shadows stretch across the floor,
Whispers echo, soft and low.
Hands of time have turned to stone,
Counting seconds, long ago.

Windows frame a world outside,
Life rushes past with fleeting grace.
Yet within, the clocks stand still,
Trapped within this timeless space.

Every tick, a memory fades,
Yet still we dream of what was lost.
In the heart of absence sings,
A clock that knows no cost.

Driftwood Dreams at Dusk

Beneath the twilight's gentle gaze,
Old driftwood tells a tale untold.
Worn and weathered by the waves,
Its spirit whispers secrets bold.

The ocean's breath, a soft embrace,
Wraps each fragment in a sigh.
Dreams arise from salty depths,
As seagulls wheel across the sky.

Each piece of wood, a journey past,
Carved by time, in nature's hands.
They linger as the daylight fades,
Carried forth by unseen strands.

In every grain, a wish remains,
To drift on waves of endless night.
With every ebb, a chance to rise,
And dance again in morning light.

Where the Mind Meets the Ether

In the stillness of the mind,
Thoughts like fireflies dance and sway.
They paint the darkness with their glow,
Creating worlds where dreams can play.

Floating on a thread of grace,
Ideas spark like shooting stars.
Each moment holds a universe,
A journey beyond earthly bars.

Whispers in the cosmic void,
Calling forth the endless themes.
Where logic bends and time dissolves,
The heart can wander through its dreams.

Here, the ether breathes alive,
Thoughts intertwine without a seam.
The mind will soar; the soul will dive,
In this place, we are but dream.

The Celestial Playground of Rest

Underneath the vast night sky,
Stars are scattered like soft sand.
Glistening in a cosmic play,
Drawing dreams to where we stand.

In this realm, our worries fade,
As the moon whispers lullabies.
Gentle breezes cradle souls,
While the universe softly sighs.

Each constellation tells a tale,
Of love and loss, of joy and pain.
We find our peace among the stars,
As time slips through a silver chain.

Here, in the silence of the night,
Our hearts can rest, our spirits soar.
In the celestial playground's light,
We dream of worlds forevermore.

The Horizon of Hidden Thoughts

Whispers in the morning light,
Dreams that dance just out of sight.
Echoes of the past still gleam,
In the heart, they softly dream.

Thoughts that linger, shadows cast,
Moments fleeting, fading fast.
On the canvas of the mind,
Hidden treasures there to find.

Questions swirl, like autumn leaves,
In the silence, calm reprieves.
The horizon beckons, waits in peace,
For the noise of thought to cease.

Pathways formed by choices made,
In the stillness, fears cascade.
With each dawn, new light is born,
On the horizon, dreams are worn.

Reflections in Night's Glass

Stars like secrets, softly shine,
In the glass of night, divine.
Moonlit whispers, tales unfold,
In shadows deep, and bright and bold.

Glimmers of the heart displayed,
In the dark, fears gently fade.
Each reflection holds a story,
Woven dreams in silver glory.

Time stands still beneath the sky,
Where the echoes dare to lie.
In the quiet, truths emerge,
As night's magic starts to surge.

Dreams float softly, like a stream,
In the night, we dare to dream.
Through the glass, we glimpse the light,
Of reflections, pure and bright.

Elysian Fields of the Subconscious

Beneath the stars, a garden blooms,
Where thought escapes and silence looms.
Fields of dreams sway in the night,
Offering solace, soft and light.

Voices whisper through the trees,
Carried on the gentle breeze.
In this realm where shadows play,
The heart finds peace, a place to stay.

Each petal holds a memory,
In the stillness, we can see.
Elysian fields, where spirits glide,
In the depths, forgotten pride.

Through the colors of the mind,
Hidden truths are sure to find.
In the subconscious, love will thrive,
As the soul begins to strive.

Breath of the Nightingale

In the twilight, songs arise,
From the heart, beneath the skies.
Nightingale, with melodies sweet,
Brings the dusk alive, a retreat.

Hushed beneath the silver light,
Every note a gentle flight.
Whispers weave through trees and air,
As the world sheds all its care.

Harmony of dreams untold,
In your breath, the night's bold.
Each refrain a soothing balm,
In the night, we find our calm.

Sing to me, O tender bird,
With your notes, my heart is stirred.
In the hush, your song will linger,
Caressed softly by your finger.

Slumbering Portals of Imagination

In twilight's soft embrace we drift,
Through portals vast, our minds uplift.
Where colors swirl and visions blend,
In dreams, we wander without end.

With whispers soft as moonlit beams,
We traverse realms of silent dreams.
Fleeting thoughts on gentle waves,
Each moment held, the heart behaves.

Beyond the veil of waking light,
The stars align in endless flight.
Through corridors of faded time,
Our spirits soar, our souls will climb.

Awake or sleep, we find our way,
In slumber's grasp, we dare to play.
So close your eyes, let visions start,
For dreams reside within the heart.

Dances in the Dreaming Dark

In shadows deep, the dancers twirl,
Their laughter echoes, soft and pearl.
With every step, the night's refrain,
Moves through the stars, a sweet domain.

The moonlight spills on velvet ground,
As magic weaves without a sound.
Each pirouette, a whispered song,
Together in the night, we belong.

Spirits rise on gossamer threads,
In mystic halls where daylight treads.
With every breath, a tale unfolds,
In rhythmic waves, the dreamer holds.

So let the darkness guide our feet,
As we embrace the night and greet.
For in this realm, both wild and stark,
We find our freedom, dancing dark.

Chasing Echoes in Night's Realm

In twilight's hush, the echoes call,
Through misty dreams, we hear them all.
In whispered tones, the night does speak,
Chasing shadows, we'll find the peak.

The cool breeze carries tales of yore,
As time unfolds, we search for more.
Each echo bounces from the past,
A fleeting glimpse that feels so vast.

With every step, the stars align,
In cosmic dance, the night is mine.
Chasing echoes, we plunge and dive,
In the realm of dreams, we thrive.

So listen close, as silence swells,
In night's embrace, our spirit dwells.
To seek the echoes, near and far,
Is to chase light, our guiding star.

The Silent Symphony of Sleep

A lullaby in shadows weave,
As slumber calls, we gently leave.
The night unfolds its tender grace,
In silent songs, we find our place.

The moonlight drapes the world in gold,
While dreams awaken, stories told.
A symphony, both soft and clear,
In every note, our hopes draw near.

With whispered chords, we drift away,
Into the realm of night's ballet.
Melodies that softly blend,
In sleep's embrace, we find a friend.

So let the music guide your rest,
In dreams, we fly, forever blessed.
For in the silence, beauty sings,
A symphony of wondrous things.

Journeys Through the Veil of Night

Whispers of shadows, soft and deep,
Footprints on paths where silence keeps.
Chasing the moon's elusive light,
Dancing with stars in the quiet night.

Voices of dusk, a calming song,
Carried by breezes, gentle and strong.
Every heartbeat, a tale to unfold,
Through layers of dreams, both new and old.

Guided by starlight, dreams take flight,
Tracing the lines where shadows invite.
In the embrace of the velvet skies,
Finding the truths that softly lie.

As dawn approaches, the night must wane,
Yet journeys through midnight, eternally remain.
In every farewell, a memory sewn,
Journeys through night are never alone.

Stars Drifting in the Sleepy Sea

Glistening gems on the ocean's crest,
Whispers of dreams in a tranquil quest.
Waves of slumber caress the shore,
As stars drift softly, forevermore.

Moonlit reflections dance and sway,
Painting the night in silvery gray.
Each twinkle a secret, a lullaby,
Sailing through slumbers, drifting high.

Ripples of night caress the sands,
Echoes of dreams slip through our hands.
In the embrace of the soft sea breeze,
Fables of starlight, eager to please.

As morning whispers, the stars take flight,
Fading away with the warming light.
Yet in our hearts, they forever gleam,
Stars drifting softly, holding our dreams.

Beyond the Close of Day

When shadows lengthen and daylight hides,
A tapestry woven where stillness abides.
Colors of twilight pool in the sky,
Promising stories as night drifts by.

Footsteps echo in the fading light,
Adventures await in the depths of night.
Each moment a page in life's winding book,
Inviting the world for another look.

The stars appear, like candles aglow,
Guiding the heart where it longs to go.
In the silence, whispers unfold,
Secrets of twilight, treasures untold.

As the day closes, new paths arise,
A canvas of dreams beneath endless skies.
Beyond the day's end, life's wonders remain,
In the twilight's embrace, we dance once again.

The Art of Forgotten Dreams

In corridors lined with faded light,
Echoes of visions take gentle flight.
Forgotten whispers, sighs from the past,
Each hidden truth, a treasure amassed.

Canvas of longing, painted in tears,
Strokes of memory, shaped by our fears.
Woven with wishes, secrets, and schemes,
Creating a tapestry of lost dreams.

In the stillness, a flicker appears,
Awakening hope buried for years.
Reviving the dreams we dared to ignore,
Unlocking the doors to hidden shores.

Through the silence, courage ignites,
Reclaiming the visions once lost to the nights.
The art of forgetting gives way to the gleam,
Of new beginnings and rekindled dreams.

A Journey Through Velvet Vistas

In valleys lush where shadows play,
A soft embrace of night and day.
Whispers call from emerald glades,
Through paths where silver moonlight fades.

The stars ignite the velvet sky,
Beneath their glow, the dreams will fly.
Each step unfolds a tale untold,
In lands where time itself grows bold.

Through azure fields of wild delight,
Where daisies dance in soft moonlight.
A journey taken hand in hand,
Among the beauty, we shall stand.

With every breath, the world anew,
In velvet vistas, pure and true.
We wander free, with hearts aflame,
And find our peace, our souls' sweet name.

The Forgotten Lanterns of Hypnos

In shadows deep where dreams reside,
Forgotten lanterns burn inside.
They flicker softly, whispers near,
A calling that we long to hear.

Through misty realms, the night expands,
Each lantern held in tender hands.
Stories untold in every glow,
Within the dark, their secrets flow.

The mind's embrace, a cozy snare,
Where slumber's kiss lingers in air.
With every sigh, the visions bloom,
In silent halls, dispelling gloom.

And as we drift through night's embrace,
Forgotten lanterns find their place.
They light the path of those who seek,
A dreamer's heart, no need to speak.

Labyrinths of the Mind's Eye

In corridors of thought we roam,
Labyrinths that lead us home.
Each twist and turn, a tale to find,
In depths entwined, we free our mind.

The echoes of the past do play,
Guiding us through night and day.
With every step, a new door swings,
Unlocking all that vision brings.

Where shadows blend with promises,
An inner world of mysteries.
We seek the light, the paths unknown,
Inside these walls, we've always grown.

The heart explores the unseen maze,
In every corner, memory sways.
Within the mind's eye, dreams connect,
A journey vast, profound and perfect.

Secrets of the Whispering Pillow

Beneath the silk, the secrets lay,
The whispered tales of night and day.
Each sigh a song, each tear a thread,
Woven closely as dreams are fed.

In twilight hours, when silence grows,
The pillow holds what nobody knows.
Soft confessions drift on the breeze,
In cozy warmth, our fears appease.

The tender weight of slumber's call,
Lulls us gently, invites us all.
In quiet corners, we let go,
And find the truths we yearn to sow.

With morning light, the whispers fade,
Yet in our hearts, the dreams are laid.
For every night that softly sighs,
The pillow keeps our sweet goodbyes.

The Language of Sleep's Veil

In shadows deep where silence dwells,
The whispers of dreams weave gentle spells.
With every sigh, the night unfolds,
A tapestry of stories told.

Beneath the stars, a soft embrace,
Time drifts slowly, finds its place.
The heartbeat of night, a lullaby,
In the arms of sleep, we softly lie.

Soft tendrils of light, they dance and sway,
Carrying our thoughts far away.
Through the veil, we softly slip,
On the ocean of dreams, we take a trip.

When morning calls, the dreams recede,
Yet in our hearts, they plant the seed.
In waking hours, their whispers stay,
The language of sleep will guide our way.

Tides of the Dreamscape

Waves of thought crash on the shore,
In the dreamscape where we explore.
Every ebb, a memory shines,
Every flow, a path unwinds.

Moonlit tides guide us through night,
In this realm of ethereal light.
Carried by currents, we drift and roam,
Finding in dreams our true home.

Shimmering visions on the swell,
Echoes of stories we yearn to tell.
The salty breeze, a whispered truth,
Awakens the spirit of our youth.

So let us dive, and let us float,
On these tides, we turn, we gloat.
For in the depths, we find our way,
In the dance of dreams, we shall stay.

Celestial Sojourns

Stars beckon us to journeys rare,
In cosmic realms, we find our care.
Galaxies swirl in a silken sea,
In the vastness, we are free.

Constellations map our dreams,
Guiding us with radiant beams.
Each twinkle holds a story bright,
In the canopy of the night.

Nebulas whisper, planets sing,
On celestial wings, we take to wing.
Time and space softly entwine,
In these sojourns, we brightly shine.

So let us wander, let us soar,
Into the heavens, forevermore.
With every star, our spirits vow,
To treasure this cosmic now.

The Enchanted Hypnos

In twilight's grasp, the world turns calm,
A lull envelops, sweet as balm.
Hypnos beckons, softly near,
Whispers of peace for hearts to hear.

In the mist where dreams reside,
The soul finds warmth, a gentle tide.
With each breath, our worries cease,
Lost in the magic, we find our peace.

The silky night wraps us tight,
Guided by the stars' soft light.
In every corner, secrets play,
In Hypnos' hold, we drift away.

As dawn draws near, the magic lingers,
In the heart's warmth, touch like fingers.
Though dreams may fade with morning sun,
The magic of night forever runs.

The Silent Symphony of Night

Stars whisper softly, in the velvet sky,
Moonlight caresses, as shadows sigh.
Crickets sing lullabies, to the stillness near,
In the heart of darkness, dreams appear.

Echoes of silence, swirl around the trees,
Rustling leaves dance, in the cool night breeze.
A symphony composed, of nature's own lore,
Each note a secret, forever to explore.

The world slows down, in this tranquil embrace,
Time feels suspended, in a sacred space.
With every heartbeat, the night draws near,
A silent symphony, only we can hear.

As dawn approaches, the notes fade away,
Yet in our memories, they forever stay.
The silent symphony, of night so bright,
Leaves us enchanted, till the morning light.

Enigmas of the Dreamscape

Wander through labyrinths, where shadows play,
Whispers of secrets, leading us astray.
Mirrors reflect, what we dare not face,
Each step a riddle, in this timeless space.

Clouds made of cotton, drift through the air,
Realities blend, in a surreal snare.
Dreamers awaken, to visions so grand,
In this enchanted, elusive land.

Time is a river, flowing undefined,
Each moment a puzzle, that fate designed.
In the realm of slumber, we laugh and cry,
As enigmas unfold, beneath a starlit sky.

Awake from the slumber, yet echoes remain,
The dreamscape lingers, like a sweet refrain.
In the heart of the night, our spirits roam,
Finding our solace, in dreams we call home.

Murmurs in the Quiet Abyss

Deep in the silence, where shadows grow,
Murmurs awaken, in the ebb and flow.
Secrets are carried, on whispers of night,
Lost in the void, yet bursting with light.

Ripples of darkness, weave through the air,
Fractured voices, in the depths we share.
Tides of emotion, pull us near,
In the quiet abyss, we confront our fear.

The calm holds chaos, beneath the facade,
Mysteries beckon, sweet whispers applaud.
Like phantoms unseen, they dance and they sway,
Guiding our hearts, as we drift away.

In this deep cavern, where silence reigns,
We capture the echoes, of joy and pain.
Murmurs of life, in stillness we find,
The quiet abyss, reveals what's entwined.

Fantasies Woven in Gossamer

Threads of desire, spun with care,
Gossamer dreams, float through the air.
In twilight's glow, where wishes unfold,
Our hearts entwined, in stories retold.

Each delicate strand, a glimpse of delight,
Wrapped in the magic of the softening light.
Visions of beauty, drift like a song,
In a tapestry woven, where we belong.

Colors of sunset, blend into night,
Fantasies shimmer, with ethereal light.
In the dance of the dusk, we lose and we find,
The essence of dreams, forever enshrined.

As dawn breaks anew, the gossamer fades,
Yet the dreams linger, in soft serenades.
Fantasies woven, with threads made of gold,
In the fabric of life, our stories are told.

Wandering Through the Halls of Morpheus

In slumber's grasp, I drift away,
Beneath a sky where dreamers play.
Echoes whisper, soft and low,
Guiding me where I must go.

Shadows dance with silken grace,
In this strange and secret place.
Faces fade like morning dew,
Lost in thoughts, both old and new.

Through corridors of choice and chance,
I follow paths, entranced in dance.
Each step a tale, a fleeting sight,
In the realms of endless night.

Awake or dream, the lines are blurred,
In Morpheus' embrace, I'm stirred.
Yet when dawn breaks, I must depart,
But carry dreams within my heart.

Celestial Shadows and Midnight Tales

Beneath the stars, the secrets lie,
Whispers of winds that softly sigh.
Celestial shadows play their game,
And midnight tales ignite the flame.

Stories etched in twinkling lights,
Of love and loss on shadowed nights.
The moon, a witness, bright and bold,
Illuminates the dreams of old.

With every tale, the night unveils,
A tapestry of shadowed trails.
Each story spun, a cosmic thread,
In the silence, soft words are said.

Underneath the sky's embrace,
We find our truth, we find our place.
With hearts aglow, we share our fears,
In celestial shadows, through the years.

The Enchanted Stillness of Night

In the hush where whispers dwell,
The night weaves its magic spell.
Stars above twinkle like dreams,
Flowing softly like gentle streams.

Moonlight bathes the world in glow,
Painting tales of long ago.
Each shadow holds a story sweet,
In the stillness, hearts can meet.

The trees sway under a silent tune,
Beneath the watchful eyes of the moon.
Crickets chirp their lullabies,
Beneath a sea of endless skies.

In this enchanted twilight space,
Time slows down, we find our grace.
Together, lost in worlds unseen,
In the stillness, we are keen.

Threads of Dreams in Tattered Sheets

In tattered sheets, dreams come alive,
Where imagination begins to thrive.
Threads of hope and whispers twine,
In the quiet, our spirits shine.

Scattered thoughts, like petals fall,
Gather close, we hear the call.
Each sigh a journey, each pause a chance,
In the tapestry of a midnight dance.

Softly weaving, night unfolds,
Tales of adventure, brave and bold.
With every heartbeat, stories start,
In the stillness, we find art.

Though dawn may break and dreams may fade,
The essence of night will never jade.
In tattered sheets, we always meet,
Where dreams are born, and shadows greet.

Fables Lurking in the Night

Whispers float on midnight air,
Tales of shadows dance and stare.
Creatures weave through moonlit glades,
Fables lost in twilight shades.

Stars above start their soft gleam,
Echoes of a forgotten dream.
Winds carry secrets, soft and low,
In the dark, their shadows grow.

A rustle here, a fleeting sound,
Mysterious stories lurk around.
Every rustling leaf has a tale,
In the night, we set our sail.

From depths of sleep, they rise anew,
Fables hidden from our view.
In the night, our fears take flight,
Illuminated by the moon's light.

Threads of Dreams Awash in Color

Painted skies in hues so bright,
Weaving dreams in soft twilight.
Threads of hope, a vibrant lace,
Gentle whispers, a warm embrace.

Colors swirl in the evening mist,
Every moment, a painter's kiss.
Palette rich, hearts intertwine,
In our dreams, the stars align.

Scattered hues of joy and pain,
Each stroke is like a sweet refrain.
Vertical lines of love and fear,
Revealing secrets we hold dear.

Drifting through this canvas wide,
Lost in color, where dreams reside.
Painting life with every breath,
Awash in shades that conquer death.

Mystical Realities of the Sleepless

In the stillness, thoughts collide,
Endless realms we cannot hide.
Whispers of the night's decree,
Mystical truths set us free.

Outside the norms, we start to soar,
Boundless journeys, evermore.
Sleepless eyes, a canvas bare,
Chasing dreams through cosmic air.

Fleeting shadows, fleeting light,
Reality bends in the night.
Floating thoughts in tangled space,
In each heartbeat, a hidden grace.

Awake to worlds where thoughts take flight,
In the darkness, we find our light.
Living visions, unconfined,
Mystical paths we choose to find.

Sleep's Tender Mirage

Softly whispers the nightingale,
Carrying dreams on a silken trail.
Sleep wraps gently like a quilt,
In its embrace, our worries wilt.

Bridging worlds with each soft sigh,
Through tender dreams, our spirits fly.
Mirages formed in moonlit streams,
Cradled sweetly within our dreams.

Echoes linger, fading slow,
To the land where wishes flow.
Each moment frozen, time stands still,
Awakening dawn yet again thrills.

Sleep may fade but love remains,
In memories, it softly reigns.
A tender mirage we cherish so,
In sleep's embrace, our hearts aglow.

Echoes from the Land of Nod

In dreams we wander, soft and free,
Through fields of stars, by moonlit sea.
Whispers of wishes dance in the night,
Carried on winds, in gentle flight.

Fleeting moments thread the deep,
Where secrets rest, and silence keeps.
In every shadow, the past will creep,
Echoes of love in the arms of sleep.

Beneath the cloak of twilight's kiss,
The world dissolves in tranquil bliss.
Thoughts like fireflies flicker and twine,
Weaving a tapestry pure and divine.

As dawn approaches, dreams take wing,
Fading softly, the night's sweet sing.
Yet in our hearts, those echoes stay,
Guiding our souls to the break of day.

Beneath the Veil of Slumber

Close your eyes as twilight lays,
A blanket of dreams in soft arrays.
The stars whisper secrets, old and wise,
Beneath the veil, where silence lies.

In the realm where shadows dance,
Every heartbeat finds its chance.
Gentle lullabies cradle the mind,
As we drift through a world unconfined.

Here in the stillness, hopes arise,
Like dawn's first light in painted skies.
Twilight unfolds its tender grace,
Awakening souls, in this sacred space.

So let the night its magic weave,
In dreams, where we dare to believe.
With morning dew, we'll greet the day,
Our spirits renewed, come what may.

Twilight's Hidden Tapestry

A canvas stretched, of dusk and dawn,
Where time and dreams are softly drawn.
Threads of silver, woven with gold,
In twilight's embrace, tales unfold.

Crimson skies with azure beams,
Softly cradle our secret dreams.
Each star a note in night's sweet song,
Calling us to where we belong.

Beneath the arches of the night,
Magic glimmers in quiet light.
As the world spins in endless grace,
In twilight's arms, we find our place.

So hush your thoughts and gently sway,
Let the night guide you on your way.
In hidden corners of the heart,
Twilight's tapestry will never part.

Nocturnal Reveries

In the hush of night, when shadows play,
Dreams take flight, weaving their way.
Soft murmurs float on the midnight air,
Calling the lost with tales to share.

Stars wink down in a silent cheer,
As heartbeats echo, drawing near.
Mysteries simmer in moon's soft glow,
Guiding us gently where we long to go.

Whispers of winds tell stories bold,
Of ancient realms and treasures of old.
In nocturnal breezes, we find our muse,
Dancing with shadows, we cannot lose.

So hold on tight to this fleeting bliss,
In every moment, find what you miss.
For in the night, our dreams take form,
As we drift through life, forever warm.

Awakenings from the Dreamer's Sea

In whispers soft, the tide does rise,
Waves of wonder kiss the skies.
With every crest, a thought does bloom,
From depths unseen, a heart finds room.

A dance of light on waters clear,
Shadows fade, and dreams draw near.
The world awakes with morning's grace,
Embracing hope in a warm embrace.

To sail the sea of dreams untold,
Where mysteries of life unfold.
In gentle ripples, truths are found,
A journey waits, forever bound.

Awakenings call, with vibrant hue,
The dreamer's quest, to seek the true.
Each wave a chance, each breath a song,
In the sea of visions, we all belong.

Constellations of the Curious Mind

In night's embrace, the stars conspire,
Each twinkle sparks a deep desire.
Maps of wonder drawn in space,
Curiosity's endless chase.

Thoughts ascend on cosmic winds,
Stories told where wonder begins.
Galaxies whisper secrets bright,
Illuminating paths of light.

Questions dance in the midnight air,
Fragments of dreams we love to share.
A tapestry of thoughts entwined,
Constellations of the curious mind.

To wander deep in realms unknown,
In realms of thought, we make our own.
With every star, a spark ignites,
Guiding us through the endless nights.

The Lure of Midnight's Call

The midnight hour sings its song,
A siren's voice, both sweet and strong.
In shadows deep, secrets arise,
Tempting hearts with whispered sighs.

Beneath the glow of the pale moon,
Desires stir, a haunting tune.
Dreamers tread with cautious grace,
In the silence, they find their place.

The lure of night, a velvet cloak,
Wrapped in warmth as spirits spoke.
Embers glow in the darkened skies,
Awakening hopes, where magic lies.

To follow where the shadows lead,
In the midnight hour, we are freed.
Each step resounds, a steady beat,
As the world pauses, life feels sweet.

Echoing Voices Beneath the Stars

In twilight's hush, the voices rise,
Echoes shimmer from darkened skies.
Beneath the stars, we share our dreams,
In whispered tones, life softly beams.

The stories told of days gone past,
In every heart, a shadow cast.
Memories dance in spectral light,
Guiding us through the velvet night.

A chorus grows from distant lands,
Bound by hopes and tender hands.
Together we stand, united strong,
In the symphony, we all belong.

So listen close, let echoes flow,
Beneath the stars, our spirits glow.
A tapestry of voices bright,
Weaving dreams in the quiet night.

Whispers of Restful Waters

Gentle waves kiss the shore,
Moonlight dances on the sea,
Softly calling memories,
Beneath the ancient tree.

The lull of night enfolds,
Echoes in the silver light,
Crickets serenade the stars,
In the stillness of the night.

Reflections of dreams untold,
Flowing with the evening tide,
Ripples weave a tapestry,
Where secrets often hide.

In the hush, a whisper swells,
Breath of life on tranquil breath,
A journey through the silence,
In the waters, find your rest.

Slumber's Ethereal Canvas

Upon the canvas of the night,
Colors blend in soft descent,
Dreams are painted, soft and bright,
In slumber's warm embrace, they're lent.

Stars like brush strokes twinkle clear,
Waves of twilight gently roll,
Whispers float, so calm and near,
As shadows cradle every soul.

Each sigh a stroke of muted hue,
In the realm where silence sings,
Visions vivid, pure and true,
In the hands of gentle wings.

Rest, sweet heart, in twilight's grace,
The night enfolds like tender lace,
In dreams, we'll meet beyond the space,
Where slumber paints our secret place.

Uncharted Territories of Night

Vast horizons stretch so wide,
Underneath a velvet sky,
Wonders lie, in shadows hide,
Where the dreams of night can fly.

Paths untraveled call us near,
Through the stillness, secrets shared,
In these lands we shed our fear,
With every step, a dream declared.

Whispers guide us, soft and low,
Through the forests deep and dark,
In the silence, wonders grow,
With each heartbeat, sparks a spark.

Lost in realms unknown, we roam,
In the depths of night's embrace,
Finding solace, finding home,
In the stars, we leave our trace.

Hushed Ballads of the Dreamcraft

In the stillness, stories spin,
Each note a woven lullaby,
Crafted softly from within,
Where the heart and shadows lie.

Beneath the arch of twilight's dome,
Hushed ballads float on evening air,
Whispered songs that guide us home,
Caressing dreams with tender care.

Fleeting moments, sweet and rare,
Dance like fireflies in the dark,
Echoes of a love laid bare,
In the quiet, gently spark.

With every strum, a path appears,
Traced in light, they softly weave,
Hushed ballads sung through gathered years,
In dreamcraft's arms, we believe.

The Slumbering Abyss

In shadows deep where silence sighs,
The moon casts dreams across the skies.
A whispered echo, soft and clear,
Awakens thoughts that drift so near.

Beneath the tide of midnight's grace,
The stars illuminate this sacred space.
With every breath, the whispers grow,
In the abyss, where secrets flow.

Embers flicker, hearts entwined,
In realms of slumber, souls aligned.
The velvet darkness, sweet and still,
Cradles gently the wandering will.

To wander where the shadows play,
In dreams' embrace, we drift away.
Through the night, a journey vast,
In the slumbering abyss, we're cast.

Twilight's Gentle Embrace

The horizon blushes, kissed by light,
As day surrenders to the night.
In twilight's arms, the world grows still,
A tranquil whisper, soft as silk.

The stars emerge, a glimmering choir,
Each note igniting the evening's fire.
The shadows stretch, and colors blend,
In this quiet hour, where dreams descend.

A gentle breeze, a lover's sigh,
As dusk unfolds the velvet sky.
In every heartbeat, time stands still,
As twilight weaves its magic thrill.

With every breath, we taste the night,
In twilight's glow, the world feels right.
A moment frozen, pure and rare,
In twilight's gentle embrace, we share.

Nocturnal Musings

When darkness falls, the mind takes flight,
In the quiet hush of the night.
Thoughts meander, like rivers flow,
In nocturnal musings, we come to know.

The world outside sleeps, unaware,
While within, our dreams lay bare.
Each fleeting thought a starry spark,
Illuminating the shadowed dark.

In moonlit corners, secrets dwell,
Whispers of stories only time can tell.
In the stillness, we find our way,
Through nocturnal musings, night turns to day.

With every sigh, we gently drift,
In the realm of dreams, we find our gift.
In this sacred hour, wild and free,
Nocturnal musings become our key.

The Depths of Dreamland

In the valleys where shadows keep,
Lie the depths where dreams do seep.
A tapestry of thoughts and fears,
Woven softly through the years.

Clouds of wonder float above,
Each a promise of gentle love.
With every heartbeat, adventure calls,
In dreamland's depths, where magic sprawls.

Through starlit paths and whispered dreams,
We chase the light in silver streams.
In the silence, enchantments bloom,
In the depths of dreamland, we consume.

Awake or asleep, we find our way,
In the embrace of night, we play.
With hearts aglow, we take the leap,
Into the depths of dreams so deep.

Riddles of the Somnolent Sea

Beneath the waves, a secret lies,
Ancient whispers meet the sky.
A dance of shadows, soft and slow,
Where tides of thought begin to flow.

Moonlit paths on sapphire beds,
Silent songs unknown, unsaid.
A treasure hunt for thoughts once lost,
In the brine, we count the cost.

Echoes of dreams on silver sands,
Carry mysteries we withstand.
Ripples play with time's embrace,
Gentle caress of nature's grace.

In twilight's hold, we'll set our sights,
On riddles woven through the nights.
The sea, a cradle of the deep,
Holds answers that we long to keep.

The Quiet Rebellion of Unseen Realms.

In shadows where the whispers grow,
A world exists we seldom know.
Flickers of light in corners tight,
Dreams break free to take their flight.

Silent tempests thrash the dark,
With quiet roars, they leave their mark.
An unseen battle brews and spins,
While outside, life quietly begins.

Hidden messages in the air,
The tapestry of thoughts laid bare.
Gentle murmurs, subtle schemes,
Revolt in silence, woven dreams.

Truth unfurling, ever bold,
Stories waiting to be told.
In unseen realms, the heart avows,
A rebellion blooms, while silence bows.

Whispers Beneath Closed Lids

As darkness falls, the world retreats,
Within the mind, a tale repeats.
Fleeting echoes softly call,
In dreams we wander, rise, and fall.

Beneath closed lids, the visions play,
Floating smoke in shades of gray.
A canvas stitched with hopes and fears,
A symphony that vanishes in tears.

In this realm of quiet grace,
We chase the shadows, find our place.
A dance of thoughts, a fleeting slide,
Where secrets of the heart abide.

In silence kept, the magic brews,
Whispers hint at hidden dues.
Awake or dream, it's hard to tell,
Beneath closed lids, we weave our spell.

Dreams Woven in Silken Threads

Stitched by starlight, soft and bright,
Dreams unfold in the quiet night.
A tapestry of hopes entwined,
Crafted whispers of the mind.

Each thread a wish, a secret shared,
In twilight's glow, we are ensnared.
Woven songs of love and loss,
Embrace the brunt, accept the cost.

In slumber's quilt, we find respite,
A dance of specters, pure delight.
And through the dark, the visions thread,
A journey born where fear has fled.

In silken dreams, we drift and sway,
On gossamer paths of night and day.
Through woven realms, with hope we tread,
In the rich fabric, our fears are shed.

The Retreat of Shadows

In twilight's hush, shadows start to fade,
Soft whispers linger where memories stayed.
The stars awaken, glimmers in their flight,
Night's gentle touch embraces the light.

Beneath the trees, secrets begin to blend,
Branches reach out, where the paths may bend.
Something stirs in the silence so deep,
Promises whisper, the night's secrets keep.

As day surrenders, the blue sky turns grey,
A tapestry woven in soft dismay.
Eclipsing the sun, shadows dance like dreams,
Their retreat a chorus, or so it seems.

Yet from the dark, a new dawn will rise,
Painting the world with gentle surprise.
The shadows may fade, but they leave a trace,
A lingering essence in this sacred space.

Floating on Moonbeams

Drifting softly on a silver glow,
The night unfolds in a soothing flow.
Each beam a pathway, a radiant thread,
Guiding the wanderer, softly it said.

Whispers of dreams dance in the still air,
Carried on beams that drift everywhere.
Eyes closed in wonder, heart wide and free,
Floating on moonbeams, just you and me.

In shadows and light, we gently collide,
Cradled by night, no need to hide.
The universe hums to a lullaby's tune,
As we twirl in the arms of the moon.

Lost in the magic, the world fades away,
Moments suspended, in sweet disarray.
Time holds its breath, as stars start to gleam,
We drift through the night, like two in a dream.

Suspended in the Quiet Dark

In the quiet dark, where silence dwells,
A symphony stirs, a tale that compels.
Time stretches onward, yet stands still,
Suspended in shadows, we feel a thrill.

Glimmers of thoughts like fireflies gleam,
Dancing through spaces, igniting a dream.
The weight of the world fades softly away,
In this breath of night, we quietly sway.

Moonlit secrets encircle the air,
Holding the weight of an unspoken prayer.
Each heartbeat echoes in rhythms profound,
Suspended in stillness, where truth can be found.

In the quiet dark, we learn how to see,
Within the abyss, we set our hearts free.
Each shadow a lesson, each sigh a release,
In the calm of the night, we discover peace.

The Echo of a Feather's Fall

A feather whispers as it meets the ground,
An echo lingers, softly profound.
It carries stories of journeys past,
A delicate dance in the autumn's blast.

Fluttering gently in the crisp air's hold,
The memory drifts, a tale to be told.
Every soft landing a moment so brief,
The world pauses, cradling its grief.

In the silence, we hear the soft sigh,
Of wings taking flight, as dreams fly high.
Yet in the stillness, the weight seems to stay,
Anchored in heartbeats that fade away.

Each echo a journey, from high to low,
Reminding us gently of what we may know.
For in every fall, there's a rise to be found,
The echo of life, an eternal sound.

Milton Keynes UK
Ingram Content Group UK Ltd.
UKHW021928011224
451790UK00005B/70

9 789916 908082